LIVING FREE

A GUIDE TO FORMING & CONDUCTING A RECOVERY MINISTRY

■■■

RON HALVORSON & VALERIE DEILGAT

Recovery Publications, Inc.
1201 Knoxville Street
San Diego, CA 92110-3718
(619) 275-1350

Published by
Recovery Publications, Inc.
1201 Knoxville Street
San Diego, CA 92110-3718
(619) 275-1350

All the scripture quotations are from the New International Version of the Bible.

The Twelve Steps have been reprinted and adapted with per-mission from Alcoholics Anonymous World Services, Inc. For purposes of this book, the word "alcohol" in Step One has been changed to read "the effect of our separation from God," and the word "alcoholics" in Step Twelve has been changed to read "others."

Published 1992
Printed in the United States of America
95 94 93 92   10 9 8 7 6 5 4 3 2 1
Distributed by The Fleming H. Revell Co.

ISBN: 0-941405-16-8 $5.95

Dedication

To all those who choose life

and recovery,

through the one true Higher Power

that makes it possible . . .

Jesus Christ.

Acknowledgement

Recovery ministries are developed to help wounded people join together in churches and experience God's love and grace. The contributions of those mentioned here do not exclude the many others who also took part in walking the path as it was being developed.

We are especially indebted to:

- Skyline Wesleyan Church staff members for their unlimited support and affirmation, and particularly Pastor Richard Hundly for his trust and belief in this material.

- Ron and Karen Martin, founders of Liontamers Ministry, for the contribution their program is making to the Christian recovery movement.

- Ron Ross, Jack McGinnis and Barbara Shlemon for publicly sharing their own woundedness.

- Dale Ryan for his support and encouragement in developing the format and content of this book.

- Participants in the recovery groups where this material was developed and tested. Their honesty and openness is greatly appreciated.

Table of Contents

Foreword

The local church is the rightful home of recovery ministry. Jesus welcomed the broken, the needy and the diseased into his fellowship, saying "those who are well don't need a physician." Fundamental to meaningful participation in the Christian community is understanding that in some sense we are not well. People struggling with the most difficult of life's dis-eases will find practical help in the Christian community, where acceptance, love and hope make change possible.

Unfortunately, many people in recovery—even Christians in recovery—feel ill at ease at church. One person said to me, "I don't know all the reasons why, but most of the time I feel 'real' at my support group meeting and I 'pretend' on Sunday mornings. I just don't feel safe to be who I really am, so I say, 'I'm fine thanks' even though it is not true." This problem is made more acute by the secular recovery community's indifference and/or hostility to Christian concerns resulting in the feeling of 'homelessness' for many Christians in recovery. They can be Christian in their church community, but their commitment to recovery will be misunderstood or unappreciated. In the recovery community, they can be in recovery but their Christian faith will be misunderstood or unappreciated.

There is good news, however. Distinctively Christian recovery ministries have developed in tens of thousands of local churches in the past decade. The impact of addiction, abuse and dysfunction on the Christian community is no longer a 'silent issue.' We are just beginning to face the truth about the extent of this impact in the local church, and just beginning to develop practical resources of genuine help for those who struggle with these difficult problems.

The *Living Free Program* is an excellent example of distinctively Christian recovery material. Ron Halvorson and Valerie Deilgat have consulted pastors and local churches on the development of recovery ministry for many years. The wisdom gained from this experience, along with their many years of personal participation in recovery, will be helpful to anyone seeking to develop a Christian recovery ministry.

May your roots sink deeply in the soil of God's love.

Dale S. Ryan

Executive Director
National Association for Christian Recovery

Preface

Ron's Story

Being in recovery from addiction, I am one of a multitude of people who owe their existence to God's grace and healing love expressed through the encouragement and support of many friends in recovery.

Much of my childhood was spent trying to survive the effects that my parents' emotional isolation, abuse and addiction had on me. Despite an early Christian influence, I soon abandoned the hope that what I learned in Sunday school would help me deal with the chaos at home. A survival decision I made in childhood was, "If it's meant to be, it's up to me." I was obsessed with a need to fill the inner emptiness that plagued me. I rationalized that if I only "got" enough or "did" enough, I would find peace.

As a child I wanted desperately to be different from my alcoholic father and not succumb to addiction. Instead, the legacy of addiction continued and, although I did not become an alcoholic, I found my own drug of choice. Adult life became a battle for survival—a battle filled with casualties. I suffered the consequences of failed businesses and marriages. I didn't want to hurt others or to be hurt, yet I was unable to see other options. I sought personal change and looked for God through New Age groups, only to find my self-defeating behavior still intact.

In my late 30's I began to understand the scope of my problems. Out of desperation, on my knees, I cried out to God for help. The God I found understood my sincerity and led me to recovery through a secular twelve step program. This was the beginning of a major transformation in every area of my life. The most significant area was in my relationship with God. Through the secular twelve step program, I was encouraged by a recovering Christian friend to accept Jesus Christ as my Higher Power.

Today, carrying the twelve-step message to hurting people is my life's work. I believe the twelve-step discipline, used within Christ-centered recovery groups, offers many alienated and wounded Christians a way to rediscover the unconditional love of God's Holy Spirit. I also believe there are seekers in secular groups who can personally experience the loving presence of God, know Christ as their Higher Power and achieve greater healing in their lives.

I've spent several years assisting Christian ministries in establishing recovery support group programs. My life has been blessed by being part of this growing network of wounded believers. This book was developed with the hope that pastors and church leaders will be encouraged to form a recovery ministry and not be hindered by the difficulties that were present in the earlier groups.

The twelve-step process of recovery is an inherently spiritual journey. It guided me from a life of confusion and grief to one of growing peace and serenity. Those changes did not happen all at once. I've learned to accept that the process takes time and patience. But God, in His time, is instilling in me the strength and character that can only come from a healthy relationship with Him.

Valerie's Story

It took the suicide of my 20-year old son to bring me to my knees and recognize the extent of my illness. My codependency was so severe that I considered rearing a family with four children, building a business, being available to all who needed me and keeping peace at any price in my home to be a normal existence. My life was spent giving myself to others, meeting their needs with no concept of who I was or what my own needs were. My main focus was to make certain that my family, friends and co-workers had their needs met.

When my son committed suicide in 1982, I was oblivious to the seriousness of his addiction and was unaware of the multiple addictions that existed in my family. This tragedy, and the gradual deterioration of our family, brought me to recovery in 1984 when a hospital psychologist informed us that we were seriously in need of recovery.

My codependency grew out of several developmental conditions. I attended Catholic school for 12 years, during the time when rigidity was present and strict adherence to the rules was expected. My father was loving and caring but demanded perfection and obedience. My mother did the best she could but was a victim of an era when wives were expected to be subservient. I was unaware of the impact that these conditions had on me until my own family began to crumble.

In spite of the negative childhood influences, I am grateful for the many gifts bestowed upon me by my parents. The most precious of these gifts are with me today and manifest themselves in my confidence and self-esteem. My ability to function in the business world as an executive and my courage to face many hardships is a result of these childhood gifts.

During my early days of recovery, I read books that felt like my autobiography, attended Adult Child of Alcoholic meetings and finally found the Twelve Steps. It was through these Twelve Steps that I was able to develop a relationship with God that I had never had in my life. My childhood concept of a fearful and punishing God was replaced by a loving God with whom I now have a nurturing relationship. It was through this transformation that I became willing to actively participate in the Christian community. I am now directing my energies toward helping wounded Christians like myself to rekindle their relationship with God.

My life continues to be full of situations that require my constant contact with God, but I know that as long as I remain committed to recovery and dedicate myself to God's will I can look forward to a life filled with peace through God's grace.

Valerie Deilgat

Chapter One

Restoring the Church as a Primary Care Giver

Ten years ago, few of us would have considered chemical dependency, sexual addiction, or eating disorders suitable topics for polite conversation within the church community. These were among the "silent issues" in the church. Today, however, addiction, compulsive behavior and abuse are widely recognized as problems of enormous personal and social significance. Consider these statistics:

- At least six million Americans are addicted to cocaine.

- Between five million and ten million are addicted to prescription drugs.

- Ten million Americans are alcoholics.

- Between 40 and 80 million people are overeaters.

- More than 50 million Americans are addicted to nicotine.

- Countless more are addicted to television, shopping, exercise, sports, and even cosmetic surgery.

- Further, it is estimated that every addict directly affects at least ten other people.

Emerging Awareness

The Christian community is not immune to these difficulties. Many life-long Christians struggle with addiction. In addition, many people come to Christ hoping to find freedom from the bondage of addiction. Often these new Christians expect their problems will immediately disappear as a result of their conversions. Eventually, however, many discover that true healing requires a lengthy process of righting the wrongs of their past.

Some of these people who suffer from addiction, compulsive behavior, or abuse find it difficult to be part of a church community. They may find that within their church, self-defeating behavior is denied, ignored, or minimized by those who use religion to shield themselves from life's realities.

Pastors and church leaders are becoming aware that there are hurting individuals within their congregation, but they sometimes lack the appropriate tools or training to cope with the problem effectively. Fortunately, more and more church leaders are developing practical programs for people who struggle with abuse, addiction and compulsive behavior. These ministries provide a safe place where individuals can begin to confront their personal difficulties.

Understanding Addiction

In contemporary life, virtually anything or anyone can become an object of addiction or overattachment. Whenever people focus obsessively on an object or compulsively search for something, they are exhibiting a strong attachment beyond the point of enthusiasm or ardent feelings. They are addicted. Looking to this self-defeating behavior for comfort and satisfaction, these individuals ultimately become separated from God, thus diminishing their spirits and impeding their freedom.

Gerald May, in his book *Addiction and Grace*, defines addiction as "any compulsive, habitual behavior that limits the freedom of human desire." May goes on to list five essential characteristics that mark true addiction. They are:

Tolerance—the phenomenon of always wanting or needing more to feel satisfied. Tolerance can be experienced either physically, as when the body adapts to increasing doses of chemical substances, or psychologically, as when people continually adjust their standard of living upward in response to increased income.

Withdrawal symptoms—reactions to the removal of the addictive behavior.

Self-deception—mental defense mechanisms such as denial and rationalization invented to counter attempts to control the addiction.

Loss of willpower—an inability to conquer the addiction despite the illusion of control.

Distortion of attention—a preoccupation with the addiction that usurps our concern for the true priorities of life, especially God. For this reason, addiction can be viewed as idolatry.

As pastors and other church leaders become aware of hurting and fragmented Christian families in their midst, they are realizing the importance of reaching out to these people. They recognize that most individuals can deny their problems for only a limited period of time. Confronting their negative behavior requires support and understanding. Through compassion and love, these hurting people can find a solution for the contradictory feelings and behaviors that accompany the pretense of always seeming "fine."

Some of these wounded Christians may fear harsh judgement for not relying on their faith in dealing with their problems. As a result, they might feel inferior and assume something is wrong with them. They may even be admonished by someone within the church community to pray and read more scripture, or to trust God more fully. As long as these people avoid their actual problems, however, the outcome can be a graceless pretense of religious life.

As more recovery programs are started in churches, a growing network of committed people are learning to build congregations that are both safe and helpful for those in recovery. Designed to assist this network of individuals, the *Living Free Program* includes practical materials that have been developed and field-tested within established Christ-centered recovery ministries. The program provides a wide range of useful resources to help organize recovery programs within churches and presents various approaches to establishing these ministries. Details of the *Living Free Program* are explained in Chapter Five.

Scripture Messages

The Bible contains several examples of dysfunction and self-defeating behavior in individuals and families, beginning with Cain slaying Abel in Genesis, Chapter Four. Cain's behavior illustrates how anger, jealousy and dishonesty can affect one's reason. When confronted with his crime and its resulting curse, Cain responded with self-pity instead of remorse. In the end, Cain became alienated from God and the land that was his livelihood.

In Genesis, Chapters 25-27, stories about Jacob and Esau remind us of the power of control and manipulation. Rebekah used her son Jacob as a pawn to deceive her husband, Isaac. In doing so, she taught Jacob to lie and deceive in order to get his father's blessing.

Many families today continue similar legacies of compulsive behavior, abuse and addiction. Adults who experienced trauma during childhood as a result of inappropriate behavior by their primary caregivers often become offenders themselves. Recent books point out the damaging effect a chaotic and unpredictable environment has on a child's development. Whether the damage was physical, psychological, or emotional, an abusive environment fosters a continuous cycle of addictive, compulsive behavior.

During his brief but powerful ministry on earth, Jesus Christ exemplified the ministry of bringing hurting people together and showing them how to love and care for one another. Later, his disciples taught these same lessons. The following scriptural passages demonstrate how Christ and his disciples conveyed these messages.

- *"Love one another."* (JOHN 13:34)
- *"Have equal concern for each other."* (1 CORINTHIANS 12:24-25)
- *"Confess your sins to each other."* (JAMES 5:16)
- *"Carry each other's burdens."* (GALATIANS 6:2)
- *"Pray for each other."* (JAMES 5:16)
- *"Encourage one another and build each other up."* (1 THESSALONIANS 5:11)
- *"Submit to one another."* (EPHESIANS 5:21)
- *"Teach and admonish one another."* (COLOSSIANS 3:16)
- *"Spur one another toward love and good deeds."* (HEBREWS 10:24)

The Holy Spirit encourages us to love, serve and care for one another. How we manifest this behavior is unique to each of us, but clear to others. As Jesus said, *"...all men will know that you are my disciples, if you love one another."* (JOHN 13:35) Through the Holy Spirit's presence, Christ-centered recovery support groups become a place where God's grace can work miracles.

Christ-Centered Recovery Support Groups

Christ-centered recovery groups enable hurting Christians to honestly share their thoughts, feelings and experiences with others from similar backgrounds. They provide a safe place for wounded people to tell the truth, talk through a crisis, openly express feelings, identify options and make decisions. They create a forum where individuals can support and encourage one another toward healing and wholeness. They also offer a safe arena in

5

which to challenge the concept that "believing is a quick fix" for life's problems. As people give up this illusion, they become more honest and aware of the denial that has protected them from the reality of their woundedness.

It is natural for people to feel comfortable and less afraid of rejection when discussing their problems and admitting their fears with others who identify with them. The process of conquering self-defeating behavior is strengthened through positive affirmation, love and support from those around them. Through this process, people can receive the comfort of God while sharing their experience, strength and hope with others.

When recovery support groups are part of a Christian community, individuals can integrate their faith in Christ with their journey toward healing. In particular, Christ-centered recovery support groups provide a safe place to:

- replace denial with honesty by being encouraged to identify destructive behavior patterns and to discover alternatives.

- comfortably share spiritual experiences with others as God leads the way through painful memories toward healthier lifestyles.

- experience the mercy and wisdom of God and the healing power of prayer by sharing personal concerns and praying for one another.

- look at hurtful experiences and unmet expectations without being ridiculed.

- learn the value of being accountable to one's self and others.

- be reminded of one's intention to stop self-defeating behavior.

Identifying the Need

After accepting the reality that woundedness exists within the church community, the next step toward addressing the problem is identifying specific needs for healing within the membership. Something as simple as an anonymous survey can reveal where to begin by identifying self-defeating behaviors, such as:

- excessive use of drugs, alcohol, or food.
- over-indulgence in sex, gambling, spending, or work.
- compulsive behavior expressed through constant volunteering, care-taking, perfectionism, or self-improvement.
- obsessive thinking about sin, weight, pornography, status, or relationships.
- unreasonable aversions to crowds, evil spirits, rejection, sex, public speaking, or disapproval.
- excessive attention and focus placed on others as a means of establishing identity and self-worth.

Based on survey results and other available information, church leaders can form Christ-centered recovery groups to address the specific needs of their community.

Recovery Support Groups

There is an important distinction between congregational care groups and Christ-centered recovery support groups. Congregational care groups are designed for people dealing with special personal problems such as grief, divorce, cancer, abortion, or single parenting. Christ-centered recovery groups focus on abstaining from self-defeating behaviors, often within a twelve-step context. This process involves developing a working understanding of the Twelve Steps as a spiritual discipline, as well as deepening one's faith and trust in God's will—an endeavor that can ultimately become a way of life. Christ-centered recovery groups combine these objectives by introducing the Twelve Steps as a tool to help participants rely on Jesus Christ for guidance in resolving troublesome personal issues.

Rooted in Christian theology, the Twelve Steps were developed in 1935 by Bill Wilson, co-founder of Alcoholics Anonymous. In the years since, these principles have been adapted to many programs which have assisted millions of people in breaking free from obsessive, compulsive behavior within the context of a renewed relationship with God. Practicing the spiritual discipline of the Twelve Steps has proven to be one of the most effective means of recovery for individuals struggling with some form of self-defeating behavior. To Christians adopting this discipline as part of their recovery program, the compatibility between the Twelve Steps and scripture is readily apparent.

Benefits of Church-Based Recovery Ministries

A number of special benefits make recovery support groups unique, including the following:

- Personal change is supported and encouraged, not demanded.

- Wounded people are able to relate to each other because of their shared life experiences.

- Scripture is used, not as a springboard for study, but to share personal lessons and experiences in light of God's word.

- Participants learn to take risks and develop trusting relationships.

Individuals suffering from the destructive effects of obsessive, compulsive behavior need to find relief. When they enter a recovery program based on the Twelve Steps, they begin a journey of Christian growth, serenity and joy. With their emphasis on spiritual renewal, the Twelve Steps provide a discipline for discovering God's healing power and are a tool to help maintain peace and serenity in an ever-changing world.

By developing a Christ-centered recovery ministry within the church, pastors and other church leaders can reach out with hope and healing to congregational members tormented by the lingering effects of an addictive or dysfunctional family environment. Christ-centered recovery support groups offer these Christians an opportunity to find peace in the fellowship of other recovering believers. In addition, these groups provide a means for congregations to join the growing recovery network within the body of Christ. In this way, the church can become a safe place for recovery.

Chapter Two

The Twelve Steps and
Their Relationship to Christianity

It is well-known that the twelve-step program developed by Alcoholics Anonymous has become the model for many other popular, lay-managed programs of treatment targeted at people with addictions, compulsions, or dependencies. These conditions include nicotine abuse, narcotics and cocaine abuse, compulsive eating and gambling. Alcoholics Anonymous estimate there are now more than 87,000 A.A. groups in 136 countries world-wide, representing 1.8 million members! Including memberships in other twelve-step programs, it can be estimated safely that millions of individuals around the world attend twelve-step meetings every week.

Alcoholics Anonymous began on June 10, 1935, co-founded by William Griffith Wilson (Bill W.) and Dr. Robert Holbrook Smith (Dr. Bob). Wilson conceived the idea of Alcoholics Anonymous while he was hospitalized for excessive drinking in December, 1934. During his hospital stay, Wilson had a spiritual experience that removed his desire to drink. In the following months, he tried to persuade other alcoholics to stop drinking just as he had. Wilson found his first "convert" in Smith, who was willing to follow Wilson's method to find freedom from alcoholism. Four years later, Wilson and Smith published the book, *Alcoholics Anonymous*, which contains the Twelve Steps and a spiritually based program of recovery from alcoholism.

The Oxford Group

Various sources influenced the formulation of A.A.'s program, as developed and recorded by Wilson. Of these, the British-born

11

Oxford Group movement and its American leader, Episcopal clergyman Samuel Moor Shoemaker, Jr., contributed most significantly to the Christian basis of Alcoholics Anonymous. Both Wilson and Smith attended Oxford Group meetings and based much of the A.A. program on this framework.

In the 1920's and 1930's, the Oxford Group movement became a revolutionary answer to anti-religious reaction following World War I. Aiming to rekindle living faith in a church gone stale with institutionalism, the Oxford Group declared itself an "organism" rather than an "organization." Group members met in homes and hotels, mingling religion with meals. Despite its freedom from institutional ties, the movement was distinctly ecclesiastical and looked to the church as its authority.

Dr. Frank N.D. Buchman, a Lutheran pastor, is most often cited as leader of the Oxford movement. Yet, if one were to ask an Oxford Group follower, "Who is your leader?" the reply might well be, "The Holy Spirit." So confidently did the group believe in the guidance of the Spirit that it had no organized board of officers, but relied instead on "God control" through men and women who had fully "surrendered" to God's will.

Buchman traveled extensively in the United States, England and the Orient, organizing local groups and urging people to follow definitive principles in order to experience a life-changing conversion. Buchman emphasized the need to surrender to God for forgiveness and guidance and to confess one's sins to God and others. Oxford Group followers learned also to make restitution for wrongs done and to witness about their changed lives in order to help change others.

The Oxford Group's teachings rested on the following six basic assumptions:

1. Human beings are sinners.

2. Human beings can be changed.

3. Confession is a prerequisite to change.

4. The changed soul has direct access to God.

5. The age of miracles has returned.

6. Those who have been changed are to change others.[1]

Ernest Kurtz, in his history of A.A. entitled *Not-God, A History of Alcoholics Anonymous* listed the following characteristics of the Oxford Group that were adapted to meet the specific needs of the A.A. program:

- informal home-like settings for meetings, intended to highlight the pleasures of spiritual fellowship;

- an expectation that members would remain in their own churches, turning to A.A. not for theological interpretations, but for support in living a moral life;

- a focus on gradually realizing a "changed life" by passing through "stages," a concept that presented sobriety as something positive rather than merely the absence of alcohol or drunkenness;

- the policy that A.A.'s workers, especially its founders, should never be paid;

- an emphasis on helping others in order to change one's own life.

In addition, Wilson incorporated into A.A.'s philosophy the Oxford Group's five procedures, which were:

1. Giving in to God.
2. Listening to God's directions.

---

(1) Cantril, Hadley, *The Psychology of Social Movements* (Huntington, NY: Robert E. Kruger, 1941), pp. 147-148

3. Checking guidance.

4. Restitution.

5. Sharing, both confession and witness.[2]

The Evolution of the Twelve Steps

While trying to attract more followers to sobriety from 1935-1937, Smith and Wilson attended Oxford Group meetings in New York led by Samuel Moor Shoemaker, Jr. "It was from Sam Shoemaker that we absorbed most of the Twelve Steps of Alcoholics Anonymous, steps that express the heart of A.A.'s way of life," Wilson later recalled. "The early A.A. got its ideas of self-examination, acknowledgment of character defects, restitution for harm done, and working with others straight from the Oxford Group and directly from Sam Shoemaker, their former leader in America, and from nowhere else."[3]

In his 1937 book, *Alcoholics Anonymous*, Wilson set forth six steps of a spiritual recovery program, based on what he and other A.A. members agreed they had learned from Sam Shoemaker and the Oxford Group. The six steps were:

1. We admitted that we were licked, that we were powerless over alcohol.

2. We made an inventory of our defects or sins.

3. We confessed or shared our shortcomings with another person in confidence.

---

(2) Kurtz, Ernest, *Not God: A History of Alcoholics Anonymous* (Center City, MN: Hazelden Educational Materials, 1979), pp. 48-49

(3) *Alcoholics Anonymous Comes of Age* (New York: A.A.W.S. Inc., 1957), p. 199

4. We made restitution to all those we had harmed by our drinking.

5. We tried to help other alcoholics, with no thought of reward in money or prestige.

6. We prayed to whatever God we thought there was for power to practice these precepts.[4]

In 1938, Wilson revised and expanded these six steps, making them more explicit in order to eliminate any possible loopholes perceived by the rationalizing alcoholic. After review and fine-tuning by other A.A. members, Wilson's revisions resulted in the Twelve Steps as we know them today. In the process, a preface was added to emphasize that the steps were intended as suggestions only. Also, in what Wilson called "concessions to those of little or no faith," God was described as a "power greater than ourselves" and "God *as we understood Him.*"

"This was the great contribution of our atheists and agnostics," Wilson explained. "They had widened our gateway so that all who suffer might pass through, regardless of their belief or lack of belief."

"God was certainly there in our Steps," Wilson continued, "but He was now expressed in terms that anybody—anybody at all—could accept and try. Countless A.A.s have since testified that without this great evidence of liberality they never could have set foot on any path of spiritual progress or even approached us in the first place. It was another one of those providential ten-strikes."[5]

As the early members of A.A. established their program's principles, they slowly began moving away from the Oxford

---

(4) *Pass It On* (New York: A.A.W.S. Inc., 1984), p. 197

(5) *Alcoholics Anonymous Comes of Age*, p. 167

Group. In doing so, however, they were not implying that the teachings of Jesus Christ were not appropriate for helping alcoholics achieve sobriety. They were, instead, attempting to make their program "available" to the largest audience possible.

In establishing the principles of A.A., Wilson borrowed material from many sources, including Christianity, and translated them into language easier for the alcoholic to accept. Consequently, A.A. members talk about spirituality, not religion; sobriety, not salvation; wrongdoing, not sin; admitting, not confessing; strength and hope, not resurrection; carrying the message, not sharing the faith. However, the absence of direct Christian references within A.A. does not take away from the program's Christian basis.

The Twelve Steps and Related Scripture

In essence, the Twelve Steps embody the Bible's core teachings concerning God's redemptive relationship with humankind, from salvation to evangelism. They begin with an admission of human shortcomings and a profession of faith in God's power, love and forgiveness—the essence of justification. The Twelve Steps go on to encourage continual confession of wrong-doing, submission to God's control and proper conduct toward others— the principles of sanctification. Finally, they encourage habits of devotion, responsiveness to God's will and sharing the message of recovery with others—the basics of biblical Christian living.

The Twelve Steps listed below have been adapted for Christians and are reprinted with permission from Alcoholics Anonymous. A corresponding scripture verse is included with each Step to illustrate the relationship between scripture and the Twelve Steps.

Step One

We admitted we were powerless over our separation from God—that our lives had become unmanageable.

"I know nothing good lives in me, that is, in my sinful nature. For I have the desire to do what is good, but I cannot carry it out." (ROMANS 7:18)

Step Two

Came to believe that a Power greater than ourselves could restore us to sanity.

"For it is God who works in you to will and to act according to his good purpose." (PHILIPPIANS 2:13)

Step Three

Made a decision to turn our will and our lives over to the care of God *as we understood Him.*

"Therefore, I urge you, brothers, in view of God's mercy, to offer your bodies as living sacrifices, holy and pleasing to God—which is your spiritual worship." (ROMANS 12:1)

Step Four

Made a searching and fearless moral inventory of ourselves.

"Let us examine our ways and test them, and let us return to the Lord." (LAMENTATIONS 3:40)

Step Five

Admitted to God, to ourselves and to another human being the exact nature of our wrongs.

"Therefore, confess your sins to each other and pray for each other so that you may be healed." (JAMES 5:16)

Step Six

Were entirely ready to have God remove all these defects of character.

"Humble yourselves before the Lord, and he will lift you up." (JAMES 4:10)

17

Step Seven

Humbly asked Him to remove our shortcomings.

"If we confess our sins, he is faithful and just and will forgive us our sins and purify us from all unrighteousness." (1 JOHN 1:9)

Step Eight

Made a list of all persons we had harmed and became willing to make amends to them all.

"Do to others as you would have them do to you." (LUKE 6:31)

Step Nine

Made direct amends to such people wherever possible, except when to do so would injure them or others.

"Therefore, if you are offering your gift at the altar and there remember that your brother has something against you, leave your gift there in front of the altar. First go and be reconciled to your brother, then come and offer your gift." (MATTHEW 5:23-24)

Step Ten

Continued to take personal inventory and when we were wrong promptly admitted it.

"So, if you think you are standing firm, be careful that you don't fall." (1 CORINTHIANS 10:12)

Step Eleven

Sought through prayer and meditation to improve our conscious contact with God *as we understood Him,* praying only for knowledge of His will for us and the power to carry that out.

"Let the word of Christ dwell in you richly." (COLOSSIANS 3:16)

Step Twelve

Having had a spiritual awakening as the result of these steps, we tried to carry this message to others, and to practice these principles in all our affairs.

"Brothers, if someone is caught in a sin, you who are spiritual should restore him gently. But watch yourself, or you also may be tempted." (GALATIANS 6:1)

Charles Knippel, Ph.D., a noted scholar on Christianity's influence on A.A., has this to say about the Twelve Steps and Christianity: "In making use of twelve-step programs and in encouraging others to use them, the Christian will view the Steps within the Christian context and give the Steps Christian meaning. In addressing himself to non-Christian members of twelve-step groups, the Christian will seek, by way of caring and sharing relationships, to bring such twelve-step practitioners to a Christian understanding of the Steps that will provide rich spiritual benefits and a more abundant experience of recovery."

"Like Sam Shoemaker, today's church leader will view Alcoholics Anonymous as a 'tutor' to bring people to Christ and His church and thus respond with a winsome Christian witness and welcome. The examination of Sam Shoemaker's theological influences on William Wilson's formulation and interpretations of the twelve-step spiritual program of recovery yields rich and life-enhancing insights for the practice of Christianity."[6]

This chapter was contributed by Bill Pittman, president of Glen Abbey Books: Author of *AA: The Way It Began* and other titles.

---

(6) Knippel, Charles, *Samuel M. Shoemaker's Theological Influence of William G. Wilson's Twelve Steps Spiritual Program of Recovery*, Ph.D. Dissertation (St. Louis University, 1987), pp. 303-304

Chapter Three

Recovery Support Group Ministries

Every day, recovering people meet at a variety of locations—churches, homes and community centers. No pre-registration is required for these meetings. Interested individuals simply locate a group that focuses on their particular problem and then attend the meeting. Group participants remain essentially anonymous; they need not reveal any personal information except their first names. During the meetings, they are free to speak openly and honestly about current issues in their lives or to remain silent and listen to others. In this environment, participants don't have to pretend their lives are perfect and free of problems.

Recovery support group meetings vary in format, cover many different subjects and utilize different types of materials. The most important factor for a person to consider in choosing a group is to find one that is compatible with his or her values and beliefs. Such a group can provide a solid foundation for initiating the healing process. Through group meetings, participants are encouraged to identify and focus on a Higher Power of their choice. There is usually little or no reference to Jesus Christ as this Higher Power.

As churches become more involved in the recovery movement, Christians are beginning to form Christ-centered recovery support groups. In these groups, Christ is identified as the Higher Power. Based on the same concepts as secular support groups, these groups constitute a voluntary social network of people organized around common needs and a process of mutual aid. Unlike secular groups, however, Christ-centered groups encourage participants to focus on Christ and his teachings as a vital part of their recovery.

Types of Christian Recovery Support Groups

Most recovery support group meetings are based on an adaptation of the Twelve Steps. Beyond this common denominator, however, meetings can vary widely. At some meetings, participants who want to talk can share thoughts and feelings with the group. At designated speaker meetings, one person speaks about an event or talks about his or her personal history. Some meetings follow a specific workbook format, while others focus on reading and discussing a pertinent book. Recovery support group meetings can be open or closed; some are open for the first several weeks and then closed to newcomers. Following is a brief description of the most common types of meetings.

Drug and Alcohol Groups

Drug and alcohol groups provide Christian love, support and direction to people suffering from chemical dependency or compulsive behavior. Participants are nurtured toward a balanced lifestyle of Christian discipleship and accountability, using scripture and the Twelve Steps as the basis for achieving sobriety and serenity.

Codependency Groups

Codependency groups provide Christian love, support and direction to those individuals who engage in compulsive behaviors which were learned by family members in order to survive in a family that is experiencing great emotional pain and stress. Participants have the opportunity to share their experience, strength and hope with one another in order to find a healthier way of living.

Adult Children Groups

Adult children groups provide a safe place for adults to become whole in Christ. Children from dysfunctional families often grow up ill-equipped for adulthood, either emotionally or spiritually. Because of their dysfunctional upbringing, they may be unable to establish a satisfying relationship with God. As a result, it is often difficult for them to realize His unconditional love and forgiveness.

General Recovery Groups

General recovery groups are designed to introduce people to the healing process and help participants discover biblical aspects of recovery. These meetings are based on four basic convictions: people are in need of recovery; recovery is a commitment to change; recovery is possible; and the Bible can be a significant resource for recovery.

Ministries for Addicts and Families

A number of ministries are available to churches planning to establish Christ-centered recovery support groups. These groups provide a wide range of methods for establishing recovery support groups in the church. Following is a brief description of some of these ministries:

Confident Kids

Confident Kids is a training program and support group that teaches healthy life skills to entire families. This ministry helps family members build self-esteem and establish a sense of mutual trust. While elementary-age children are learning positive behaviors through games, skits, prayer and small group discussion, parents are instructed to encourage these behaviors at home. The program strengthens each participant's relationship with God and teaches them to use prayer and scripture as resources in dealing with life circumstances.

Freedom Weekend / Bring the Children, Inc.

Freedom Weekend is a shared experience of healing for individuals who grew up in a family where alcohol or other dysfunctional behavior existed. It is also for those whose childhood included painful loss, trauma, or broken relationships with these primary caregivers. The weekend is conducted by Father Jack McGinnis, a recovering person who shares openly and honestly about his own brokenness and journey of grieving and healing. The program is offered in the United States, Canada and England, or through a twelve-session video program with an accompanying workbook for individuals and groups. This video program is entitled *The Truth Will Set You Free*, and is co-authored with Barbara Shlemon.

Kingsland Baptist Church

Kingsland Baptist Church is a pioneer in bible-based ministries for adult children. Located in Houston, Texas, this rapidly growing church conducts several meetings including share groups, open meetings, Sunday school classes and two annual retreats. Dr. T.D. Sledge, pastor, has delivered several series of messages as part of his personal pilgrimage in facing his past as a child of an alcoholic. Some of these messages are part of a tape series produced by Giant Step Productions.

Liontamers

Liontamers is a twelve-step Christian support group designed to help recovering addicts and people from addictive or dysfunctional families deal with significant issues that are interfering with their lives. Their goal is to provide hurting Christians with hope, inspiration and a positive approach to recovery. Liontamers leaders conduct recovery support group meetings, train group leaders and facilitators, and willingly share their faith and vision with others in recovery.

Living Free

Living Free is a series of Christ-centered support group meetings designed by and for people reared in an addictive, emotionally repressive, or dysfunctional family. The program is designed to help pastors and church leaders support hurting people within their congregation. The materials provide participants with tools to develop behaviors that promote a healthy, positive lifestyle. More information on this program is contained in Chapter Five.

Overcomers Incorporated

Overcomers Incorporated is a Florida based network of more than 100 ministries offering support groups, family education seminars and outpatient counseling to Christians reared in an addictive or dysfunctional family. Although each ministry is independent, leaders meet together bi-monthly in regional gatherings to discuss issues that arise in their respective ministries. This network works closely with Faith Farms and Dunklin Memorial Camp, facilities which have provided hope and direction to alcoholics and addicts for over 40 years.

Overcomers Outreach

Overcomers Outreach is a lay ministry consisting of support group meetings within evangelical Christian churches. This ministry includes twelve-step support groups designed to combat the fear, guilt, anger, loneliness, confusion and frustration experienced by addicts, chemical dependents and their families. These groups allow individuals to study the Twelve Steps and related scripture, share experience, strength and hope, and pray specifically for each other's needs. There are numerous meetings throughout the United States.

Recovery Works!

Recovery Works! is a ministry that offers various twelve-step recovery programs, including meetings, dinner fellowships, Bible studies, conferences, lectures and retreats. This ministry focuses on educating and supporting those who wish to actively pursue recovery through the spiritual discipline of the Twelve Steps, in light of God's revelations in Jesus Christ. An adapted version of their meeting format is included in Chapter Six and is the format used for the Living Free Primary Level Open Meeting.

Skyline Wesleyan Church

Skyline Wesleyan Church sponsors various Christ-centered recovery programs and congregational care support groups in San Diego, California. The program is extensive and covers a wide range of topics, including "Cancer Care," "Foster Parents" and "Starting Over Single." In addition to this curriculum, they offer the *Living Free Program* as described in Chapter Five.

Additional Resources

The following resources provide support to individuals establishing or participating in Christ-centered recovery support groups. They contain practical, useful information for Christians on the path toward healing and wholeness.

National Association for Christian Recovery (NACR)

NACR is a ministry of the Recovery Partnership, a non-profit, corporation with headquarters in Whittier, California. The association encourages the development of organizations that seek to provide the church with Christ-centered and outreach-oriented recovery strategies. NACR helps Christians integrate recovery with faith and provides support for those involved in the growing recovery network. The organization publishes *Steps*, a quarterly magazine containing information on Christian support groups, workshops and conferences. Special attention is given to profiles of Christians in recovery, Bible study aids, and book reviews.

Edge TV

The Edge TV video club is for youth pastors working with adolescents who are struggling with complex issues they encounter daily. Topics include personal image, sexuality in its many manifestations, relationships with God and others, substance abuse and addictive/compulsive behaviors. Each video contains a segment with a personality who could be recognized by teens and who shares personal experiences of brokeness and healing through God's grace. Each 45-minute video consists of five stand-alone segments, each of which is shown and discussed separately. The segments are six to twelve minutes in length and are used as a way to encourage discussion within the group.

2100 Productions

2100 Productions produces videos which are designed for use with student groups, churches, conferences, camps and schools. They are part of InterVarsity Christian Fellowship, a student movement active on college campuses. Productions include:

- *Ripped Down the Middle* addresses the problems of growing up in an addictive or dysfunctional family and offers hope for healing. The video is designed to help individuals become the kind of healthy, well-adjusted people God intended them to be. A group discussion guide is included.

- *Picking Up the Pieces* confronts misunderstandings that people may have about serving God and ministering to others. This video helps individuals face brokenness that results from a variety of family or societal abuses. Discussion questions are included.

Resource List

Confident Kids
720 W. Whittier Blvd. #H
La Habra, CA 90631
(213) 697-6201
FAX (213) 694-6930

Dunklin Memorial Camp
3342 S.W. Hosannah Lane
Okeechobee, FL 34974
(407) 597-2841

Edge TV
P.O. Box 35005
Colorado Springs, CO 80935
(800) 366-7788

Faith Farms
9538 Highway 441
Boynton Beach, FL 33436

Freedom Weekend/
Bring the Children, Inc.
2737 Buffalo Speedway #210
Houston, TX 77098
(713) 623-2737

Giant Step Audio Productions
(Recovery Audio Tapes)
P.O. Box 471
Barker, TX 77431
(713) 492-0845

Kingsland Baptist Church
20555 Kingsland Blvd.
Katy, TX 77430
(713) 492-0785

Liontamers
2801 N. Brea Blvd.
Fullerton, CA 92635
(714) 529-5544

Living Free
1201 Knoxville St.
San Diego, CA 92110
(619) 275-6639
FAX (619) 275-5729

National Association for
Christian Recovery
721 W. Whittier Blvd. #H
P.O. Box 11095
Whittier, CA 90603
(310) 697-6201

Overcomers, Inc.
4235 Mt. Sterling Avenue
Titusville, FL 32780
(407) 264-0757

Overcomers Outreach, Inc.
2290 W. Whittier Blvd.
La Habra, CA 90631
(213) 697-3994

Recovery Works!
2737 Buffalo Speedway #210
Houston, TX 77098
(713) 621-2552

Skyline Wesleyan Church
1345 Skyline Drive
Lemon Grove, CA 91945
(619) 460-5000

2100 Productions
P.O. Box 7895
Madison, WI 53707-7895
(800) 828-2100
(608) 274-9012

Chapter Four

Forming a Recovery Ministry

Recovery support groups are unique; they involve various legal, financial and emotional aspects that do not always apply to Bible studies or congregational care groups. Consequently, pastors, counselors and other church leaders interested in forming a recovery ministry within the church need to understand the function and objectives of these groups.

Church leaders must first learn the basic principles of recovery support groups and how these groups can help their hurting members. When pastors are familiar with the concepts and processes involved, they can better identify individuals in need of recovery and respond with support and encouragement to those who wish to integrate recovery with their faith.

Building the Foundation

When beginning a recovery ministry, it is important to identify issues that need to be addressed. Usually, these issues stem from a myriad of past or present events and circumstances. They include chemical dependency, eating disorders and emotional damage caused by incest, violence, living with an alcoholic, or growing up in a dysfunctional family.

The need for recovery support groups within the church can be identified in various ways, including a survey to determine the specific needs for healing within the membership. Refer to page 73 in the Appendix for a sample survey. Pastors and church leaders can also talk with their parishioners to uncover relevant issues. After these needs are identified, church leaders can then meet with members to discuss their concerns and establish goals for a recovery ministry. Asking for congregational

29

support will encourage individuals who are already in recovery programs to help organize Christ-centered support groups.

Church Leadership and Support

Support and encouragement from pastors and church leaders are fundamental requirements for a successful recovery program within the church. When congregational leaders understand the concept of recovery and provide a solid foundation for its incorporation into the church, hurting members are often more receptive toward the program. They feel more secure in pursuing recovery if they believe church leaders understand their dilemma and are willing to support them.

Even without actively participating in recovery support group meetings, pastors and church leaders can have a powerful impact on their success by:

- sharing personal life experiences, even if they are not directly related to recovery issues;

- joining the National Association for Christian Recovery (NACR), an organization that supports recovering Christians and provides valuable tools to help them integrate recovery with faith;

- providing educational opportunities through books, videos, or other visual aids for those who want to start a recovery ministry or participate in one;

- organizing educational workshops with recovery-related themes such as "Improving Self-Esteem" or "Recognizing Denial;"

- arranging recovery-related Sunday school lessons, such as "Identifying Codependent Behaviors" or "Healing the Brokenness of Our Past;"

- developing materials that introduce young people to recovery issues;

- being available to discuss problems with recovering Christians or direct them to professional counseling if it appears necessary;

- arranging for church members to give testimonies of their own recovery experiences as part of the worship services;

- being aware of the pain involved when individuals begin to confront their past and make changes in their behavior and circumstances; and

- presenting a series of sermons on understanding the twelve-step discipline, explaining how God uses the process to manifest His healing power.

Legal Issues

There is an important distinction between church-sponsored recovery support groups and similar outside groups that only rent meeting space from the church. It is extremely important that church leaders understand the church's legal responsibility regarding each of these types of meetings.

When a church rents space to outside groups such as Alcoholics Anonymous, Al-Anon, or Codependents Anonymous, the need for personal liability coverage is minimal. The only requirement is protection against accidents or injuries while people are on the premises. The church is not responsible in any way for the reactions or behavior of any individual that may result from participation in a recovery meeting.

Church-sponsored recovery groups are a different matter. Pastors and leaders need to know that the church may be held liable for an individual's destructive behavior occurring as a result of these meetings. Concerns about potential liability should be discussed with a lawyer and an insurance professional. An

31

example of a legal opinion regarding Church liability is included in the Appendix.

To help minimize the risk of litigation, group leaders should stress that Christ-centered recovery meetings are not to be confused with group therapy or professional counseling sessions. Psychologists, therapists and counselors are committed by law to a professional standard of behavior while counseling others. Group members should understand that support group facilitators do not assume a professional role, and group processes are not intended to imitate methods used by these licensed professionals. The purpose of these groups is not to offer advice, but rather to provide spiritual guidance and support to participants dealing with painful life issues. There is no charge for participation. By tradition, recovery groups are self-supporting. Participants are collectively responsible for expenses incurred, such as rent, materials and refreshments.

To further guard against legal difficulties, recovery group participants should never be advised to perform a particular act or to refrain from doing something. Statements such as, "Leave your drunken husband if he comes home again in that condition" or "Don't waste your energy getting angry—it just makes matters worse" are inappropriate in recovery group settings. However, it is acceptable to assist a woman in coping with her drunken husband by strengthening her spiritually through prayer and encouraging her to seek professional guidance if necessary. Individuals can also be encouraged to honestly express their thoughts and feelings to other group members. Ministry leaders should be familiar with agencies that can provide help when a circumstance goes beyond the functions of a recovery support group or the responsibility of church staff.

In conducting support group meetings, it is important to further maintain the distinction between group processes and professional counseling by using religious and recovery terms instead of professional phraseology. It is appropriate, for example, to refer to individuals as meeting participants, group members, or ministry students instead of clients; to use the term prayer group or support group instead of group therapy; and to offer spiritual guidance and support instead of advice.

Finally, when a recovery support group functions as part of a church ministry, both the leader and group members are expected to act appropriately. Regular meetings held between church leaders and group leaders can be an important communication tool that helps to keep problems from becoming unmanageable.

Common Characteristics of Recovery Support Groups

Christ-centered recovery support groups are intended to provide a safe place where individuals can share their thoughts, feelings and experiences with others. They create an atmosphere where people from similar backgrounds can learn to replace denial with honesty and thus begin to confront their negative behavior. This process offers individuals an opportunity to recover from the effects of their self-defeating behavior.

Within the group setting, participants are considered equals. Titles, degrees, or other factors that could foster a pecking order within the group should be minimized so that individuals can communicate as peers and learn to develop healthy, functional relationships.

As members become better acquainted and more comfortable with one another, they can try out new behaviors within the safety of the group. By learning to respect one another, participants can take emotional risks through honest sharing and thus benefit from loving experiences. Through this process, every member is given an opportunity to testify to the love of Christ.

For many Christians, the church environment has provided a mask behind which they can hide from reality and pretend that life is free of problems. These individuals may have been led to believe that the Christian faith is a "quick fix" for life's difficulties, that all one has to do is believe, and problems will disappear. Within the group setting, however, people come to realize that struggles are natural, that God did not intend for us to lead an uncomplicated life. Even Jesus experienced days of discomfort and weariness when everything seemed hopeless.

Support group leadership is group-centered. A facilitator should provide overall guidance to keep the meetings running smoothly. This person offers support and direction to meeting participants and serves as a resource for answering questions relative to the material.

Facilitator Qualifications and Responsibilities

Experience has shown that recovery support groups benefit significantly when led by a recovering person with an understanding of twelve-step materials and experience in leading recovery support group meetings. Someone who has attended other support group meetings understands group dynamics and processes and can extend this knowledge to others. An experienced facilitator offers group members an element of security by being available and aware of what to do when problems arise. Facilitators can become acquainted with participants by interacting with the group members each week.

When selecting a facilitator it is recommended to choose an individual who has:

- an understanding of twelve-step principles and traditions and a working knowledge of twelve-step programs;

- an understanding of dysfunctional behaviors and their origins and effects;

- a God-given desire to serve the Lord by helping others confront and overcome their problems; and

- a lifestyle consistent with Christian principles.

The Facilitator is responsibile to:

- provide a positive example of working toward recovery by honestly facing and dealing with personal issues;

- moderate the meetings and ensuring that they start and end on time;

- help weekly leaders to resolve difficulties within the group; and

- help to provide a loving, trusting environment that encourages sharing and caring.

It is important for participants to understand that a facilitator cannot give professional advice, but is available to share his or her own experience, strength and hope. When a professional therapist, counselor, or psychologist facilitates a recovery group, he or she must be willing to participate on the same level as other members and not in a professional capacity. A facilitator shares personal experiences and faith, as blessed by God's grace. This person does not dominate the meeting, but gently guides its progression so that everyone can experience discovery and healing. It is important for all concerned to remember that God is guiding the entire recovery process; He is the ultimate authority within the group.

Recruiting Participants

Starting a recovery ministry within the church is not difficult. It can be successfully integrated into the lives of church members simply by inviting interested parties to participate. The program can be publicized in church bulletins or newsletters and through announcements at church meetings, including Sunday school and worship services. In addition, announcements at secular support group meetings give Christians attending those meetings an opportunity to join a Christ-centered group. Further discussion on recruiting participants is included in Chapter Six.

Chapter Five

The Living Free Program

The Living Free Program provides curricula for a series of Christ-centered support group meetings designed by and for people raised in addictive, emotionally repressive, or dysfunctional families. After attending secular support groups, the developers of the Living Free Program recognized the need for similar groups within the church. Consequently, they created this ministry to provide a Christ-centered recovery program for those who recognize Christ as their Higher Power.

The program provides a way for churches to become part of the growing recovery network. It is designed to help pastors and other church leaders support hurting people in their congregations. The program offers help to those in the church who, despite their best efforts, continue to battle painful issues stemming from past or present circumstances.

Courses offered through this program create a safe environment where participants can learn to establish and maintain a loving relationship with God, themselves and others. Living Free Program materials emphasize the importance of God's healing grace as part of the recovery process and provide a comfortable way for wounded Christians to discover areas in their lives that require healing. The program involves four levels. The Primary Level consists of an open meeting format for individuals who prefer to share in a manner similar to open meetings in codependency, adult children of alcoholics and drug or alcohol recovery support groups. The courses offered in Levels One, Two and Three begin with an introductory meeting to familiarize participants with materials, course format and specific procedures. Program materials incorporate an adapted version of the Twelve Steps of Alcoholics Anonymous with scripture and prayer. Using these tools, participants can develop behaviors that promote a healthy, positive lifestyle. The course format includes group communication, which allows individuals to share their experience, strength and hope with one another. Involvement in this program prepares people to use the Twelve Steps as a spiritual discipline, with emphasis on Christ-centered recovery. A suggested program calendar is included at the end of this chapter.

Family Groups

An important element of any recovery ministry is that people must feel secure within their group. Consequently, the group meetings outlined in the Living Free Program offer participants the opportunity to share their thoughts and feelings in small sub-groups or "family groups." This style of interaction allows group members to develop close relationships with a limited number of people in a trusting and safe environment. A small group atmosphere encourages healthy, nurturing, family-type communication among participants. It provides a safe atmosphere where trust can be developed and serves as an arena for quality sharing. These small family groups are similar to sponsorship in secular Twelve Step support groups. They provide an opportunity for participants to develop a special relationship with at least one other person

As individuals share their early experiences of growing up in an emotionally repressive or troubled family, they begin to identify the damage that has been done and recognize the need for healing. After a few meetings, they may be able to express long-suppressed shame, anger, fear and guilt, opening a pathway for God's healing grace.

Living Free Curricula

Living Free Program sessions are offered on four ascending levels. The curricula includes materials for individuals just learning about recovery, as well as for people in recovery who are familiar with twelve-step programs. Each level helps individuals increase self-esteem and effectively cope with various issues that negatively affect their lives. Program participants can gain valuable insight about themselves, while learning how to identify and confront significant issues in their lives. With the grace of God, hurting Christians participating in the Living Free Program can gradually move from pain and denial toward healing and wholeness.

Primary Level: Open Meeting

The Primary Level meetings are conducted weekly on an ongoing basis. Individuals are invited to attend these meetings before making a commitment to the more structured meetings in Levels One, Two and Three. These meetings are helpful for individuals who are just beginning recovery. They may still be identifying codependency or adult child issues and are not ready to make a commitment to participate in the more structured program. Primary Level meetings are also helpful for those who wish to attend more than one meeting weekly. The meeting format is adapted from the format used in Recovery Works! ministry, and is included in Chapter Six, page 58. This course is offered on a different day or at a different time than the other courses to allow participants to attend other meetings.

Level One: Introduction to Recovery Issues

Level One of the Living Free Program introduces participants to fundamental issues common to individuals in the beginning stages of recovery. Each Level One course emphasize relying on God's healing power as part of the recovery process. Participants are gently encouraged to examine many of the painful issues common to adults reared in addictive, emotionally repressive, or dysfunctional environments. These issues include codependency, denial, shame and grief.

Each Level One session includes writing exercises and an opportunity for individuals to share their experiences within a small family group setting. Time is allotted during each meeting for prayer requests. Completion of one of these initial courses is required before participants may enroll in Level Three. The materials used in Level One are:

When I Grow Up...I Want To Be An Adult
by Ron Ross

This introductory 12-week course was designed for Christians reared in an addictive or dysfunctional family. It offers participants a gentle way to begin the healing process through Christ-centered recovery. Based on the author's personal experiences, the workbook for this course provides hope and direction for working through the pain and frustration resulting from a traumatic upbringing. It clearly defines the characteristics of adult children and guides the reader toward a healthier lifestyle. The book also outlines methods for identifying symptoms of emotional pain and helps individuals bring healing home to family, friends and loved ones. Instructions for facilitating and conducting these meetings are included in the book's Appendix.

The Truth Will Set You Free
by Father Jack McGinnis and Barbara Shlemon, R.N.

This video series and companion workbook touches hearts and illustrates the healing power of Christ. The 13-week course is intended for adults who still suffer from childhood wounds resulting from the dysfunctional behavior of their primary caregivers. This material helps individuals work through unresolved grief and codependency issues in a gentle, loving way.

By sharing their own experience, strength and hope, the authors provide valuable insight on achieving peace and serenity through the recovery process. They encourage hurting Christians to move toward freedom and wholeness by facing their grief, shame and denial. Instructions for conducting and facilitating these meetings are included in the book's Appendix.

(Note—This course requires the purchase of one video set for group use. One workbook is included with each set. Additional workbooks are available separately in any quantity.)

> ## *Level Two: Introduction to the Twelve-Step Recovery Process*

Level Two materials introduce the twelve-step process as a spiritual discipline and clearly illustrate the compatibility between Christianity and the Twelve Steps. This course also offers participants an opportunity to share their thoughts and feelings in a support group setting, and it does not include writing exercises. Level Two repeats every 13 weeks with a one-week break and can be attended while enrolled in Level One classes. This course is offered on a different day or at a different time than the other classes to allow participants to attend each meeting. Participation in this course is recommended prior to beginning Level Three. The book used in Level Two is:

The Twelve Steps for Christians
by Friends in Recovery

This 12-week course provides an important foundation for completing Level Three. The main objective of this material is to examine the healing power of the twelve-step process when applied within a Christian perspective. Written by and for individuals who have experienced childhood trauma or deprivation, the book includes scriptural passages that illustrate the compatibility between Christianity and the Twelve Steps.

With God's grace, this course helps participants maintain balance and order in their lives through the use of the Twelve Steps.

Level Three: The Twelve-Step Journey To Wholeness

Participants in this course learn to use the Twelve Steps as a tool for examining their self-defeating behaviors and as a basis for making positive changes in their lives. They also receive an opportunity to deepen their relationship with God and develop a better understanding of themselves and those around them. The book used in Level Three is:

The Twelve Steps—A Spiritual Journey
by Friends in Recovery

This extensive 27-week course presents the twelve-step process as a spiritual journey toward healing from childhood traumas and self-defeating behaviors. Participants are encouraged to read each chapter and complete written exercises prior to attending each meeting. The book contains weekly exercises to be completed within small family groups during the meetings. Biblical references aid Christians in confronting their past and surrendering their lives to God as part of the recovery process. Instructions for facilitating and conducting these meetings are included in the book's Appendix.

Principles and Guidelines for Recovery Support Group Meetings

Christ-centered recovery support groups should establish certain principles as part of their pattern for conducting meetings. The following five principles should be honored each time the group meets:

■ Provide a non-threatening system of mutual accountability.

- For example, one member can call another each day for prayer and support in abstaining from a harmful habit. The person being supported can both give and receive strength and courage by reporting the results to the whole group.

■ Minister to specific areas of need with directed group prayer.

- Openly sharing thoughts and feelings with trusted and supportive friends helps to clarify specific needs and focus prayer on problem areas.

■ Minister to each person in the group according to his or her own needs.

- Participation in recovery support groups can help people free themselves from the past, live honestly in the present and develop realistic expectations, plans and goals for the future. Recognizing another's needs helps people to be supportive and understanding when others are sharing their experiences.

■ Encourage one another to progress from a state of physical, emotional and spiritual sickness to wholeness of life.

- Individuals need others to support them as they move from a comfortable place to a less comfortable place where change is possible.

- Aid one another in applying biblical truths to personal and relationship needs.

  - When group members openly share their faults with one another, honesty, trust and healing occur.

When clear guidelines are established for group participation, members know what to expect during meetings. This is an important factor for people who were reared in addictive or dysfunctional families where agreements were vague, rules were unspoken, or boundaries were absent.

Experience has shown that the following guidelines aid Christ-centered recovery groups in promoting integrity, maintaining consistency and ensuring a healthy supportive process.

The facilitator should:

- Support open communication among participants by:

  - truly listening to what is said,

  - encouraging expression of ideas and feelings,

  - exercising patience and empathy, and

  - rewarding honesty and openness with affirmation.

- Promote a sense of unity within the group by:

  - encouraging members to rely on Jesus Christ as their Higher Power,

  - focusing on harmony as a priority in the group process, and

  - encouraging appropriate trust and loyalty.

- Demonstrate recovery-type sharing by:

  - relating to group members at their level of recovery,

  - promoting sharing on a feeling level, and

- using personal experiences as a means to communicate ideas and feelings.

■ Make an effort to resolve conflicts by:

- confronting in a loving way,

- encouraging honest and open communication,

- providing a non-threatening atmosphere in which individuals can share their discomfort, and

- openly discussing difficulties that may arise when individuals do not honor group guidelines.

A facilitator should also be particularly sensitive to group members who may experience stress or discomfort as a result of group participation. When people touch on painful issues, especially for the first time, they may become emotional and begin to cry. The facilitator and other group members should be patient, accepting the participant's sadness as a natural and appropriate part of the healing process and allowing them to release their emotions. Rather than interrupt the session, the facilitator should ensure that sharing continues. If the situation appears serious, the facilitator should urge the individual to seek professional help.

Group participants should:

■ Come to each meeting prepared and with a prayerful attitude.

- Before each meeting, read designated materials, complete any written exercises, pray for guidance and a willingness to share openly and honestly and communicate with at least one other group participant.

- Maintain confidentiality.

  - Keep whatever is shared within the group to ensure an atmosphere of safety and openness.

- Refrain from gossip.

  - Feel free to share your own needs, but refrain from talking about a person who is not present.

- Encourage comfort and support by sharing personal experience, strength and hope.

  - Support others without attempting to advise or rescue them. Often at least one other person in the group has worked through a similar struggle and can offer hope of success.

- Make a point of ministering love in an appropriate manner.

  - Respect the needs of others by asking permission before communicating concern with a hug or touch. Many people are not familiar or comfortable with expressions of love or affection that involves physical contact.

- Refrain from criticizing or defending other members.

  - Lovingly hold others accountable for their behavior only if they ask you to do so. Otherwise, recognize that we are all accountable to Christ, and it is not our place to defend or criticize others.

- Limit talking and allow others to share.

  - Keep your comments brief, take turns talking and don't interrupt others.

- Recognize that the Holy Spirit is in charge.

  - Realize that the leader is merely a facilitator. Gratefully acknowledge the Holy Spirit's presence and pray for His guidance and discretion.

■ Refrain from "crosstalk."

- Crosstalk occurs when two or more people engage in a dialogue that excludes other participants and becomes advice-giving. Accept what others say without comment, realizing it is true for them. Assume responsibility only for your own feelings, thoughts and actions.

Suggested Program Calendar

Weeks	Primary Level ONGOING OPEN MEETING	Level One		Level Two THE TWELVE STEPS FOR CHRISTIANS	Level Three THE TWELVE STEPS—A SPIRITUAL JOURNEY
		WHEN I GROW UP...I WANT TO BE AN ADULT	THE TRUTH WILL SET YOU FREE		
1-4					
5-8		12 Weeks		12 Weeks	
9-12					
13-16					
17-20			13 Weeks	12 Weeks	
21-24					
25-28					28 Weeks
29-32					
33-36		12 Weeks		12 Weeks	
37-40					
41-44					
45-48			13 Weeks	12 Weeks	
49-52					
53-56					
57-60					
61-64		12 Weeks		12 Weeks	
65-68					28 Weeks
69-72					
73-76			13 Weeks	12 Weeks	
77-80					

Chapter Six

Organizing and Conducting the Living Free Program

The following schedule is a six-week plan that can serve as a guide in establishing a recovery support group program. Prior to formal planning, hold an exploratory meeting with individuals who are willing to support a recovery ministry. This initial gathering can help in identifying possible co-facilitators and others in the church who are familiar with twelve-step programs. It can also help in determining recovery issues to be addressed. During the process, pray that God will direct decisions and inspire people to become involved.

Develop the Foundation

■ Meet with the pastor or leader who is responsible for coordination to discuss the need for a recovery support group ministry.

■ Select a group facilitator who meets some of the following qualifications:

- Prior or concurrent participation in the recovery process through a twelve-step program such as substance abuse, eating disorders, codependency, adult children of alcoholics, or sexual abuse.

- A minimum of one-year abstinence from mood-altering substances.

- Familiarity with group leadership or experience in leading a recovery group.

49

- An understanding of the dynamics of recovery that includes setting appropiate boundaries and developing healthy interdependent relationships.

■ Prepare and distribute a congregational survey to determine the issues that need to be addressed in the meetings. Refer to the sample survey included in the Appendix.

- Determine how it will be circulated to selected groups in the church and within the community. Plan to collect all surveys by the end of week two.

■ Develop the organizational aspects of the group.

- Set a starting date, day and time of the meeting. Allow adequate time to process survey information and circulate publicity announcements.

- Resolve any concerns about group process or content, especially the concept of peer leadership and the use of materials that focus on finding healing through practicing one's faith.

- Obtain a meeting room and plan a comfortable seating arrangement.

- Plan simple refreshments.

- Arrange for child care if it is to be made available.

■ Develop a plan to publicize the meetings.

- Prepare a written announcement that includes a description of the group, the date and time of the meeting, and other pertinent information. Sample meeting announcements are included at the end of this Chapter.

- Prepare an announcement to be read during church services.

- Arrange for testimonies to be presented to interested church groups by facilitators and/or key program support people.

- Develop a plan for introducing the issues of recovery to the congregation.

- Arrange with the pastor to present a sermon that relates to the the topics to be addressed by the group, or a broader message on healing the brokenness of our past.

Develop the Program

■ Meet with the pastor or support group coordinator to review the results of the congregational survey.

- Begin planning the Primary Level open meeting and Level One classes.

- Determine the topics to be covered in the Level One meeting and select the appropriate book(s) from the Living Free Program materials. The books in this level include *When I Grow Up...I Want To Be An Adult* and *The Truth Will Set You Free*.

■ Create a calendar to determine the dates and sequences of the courses to be offered on all levels. A sample program calendar is included at the end of Chapter Five.

■ Order the books required and make announcements that the meetings are starting. A sample meeting announcement for each course is included in the books that will be used. Study the introductory material and meeting format included in the selected materials. An abbreviated meeting announcement is included at the end of this Chapter.

- If assistance is needed during the planning process, please call (619) 275-6639 and ask for information on the Living Free Program.

51

Publicize the Meetings

- Publicize the meetings that will be starting and distribute announcements.

- Establish dates for testimonies and sermons.

- Set a date for presenting the concept of recovery, which can include a Sunday school panel discussion on family dysfunction, codependency, or addictive/compulsive behaviors.

- Arrange a meeting to establish a core support group of people who are willing to help during the meetings. Invite people who have participated in twelve-step recovery programs to attend. Encourage them to support the new recovery ministry and serve as a resource to newcomers.

Prepare For the First Meeting(s)

- Review the Primary Level Meeting Format that is included on page 58 or the meeting format in the Level One book selected for review. Follow the instructions for the introductory meeting that are included in the materials.

- Visit the meeting location and arrange for sufficient chairs, a table for refreshments, and a television/VCR if required.

- If necessary, make signs to direct people to the room.

- Confirm child care arrangements.

- Obtain supplies needed for refreshments.

- Contact core support group members to confirm their involvement and availability. Meet with them to review the ground rules for the meeting as outlined in the selected text.

- Organize meeting supplies, including name tags, pencils, papers and 3x5 cards.

- Clarify any questions regarding the meeting format.

Day of First Meeting

- Arrive one hour before the meeting to arrange the room and prepare the refreshments.

  - Review the requirements for conducting the first meeting and ask for help if needed.

  - Greet all who attend and distribute the required materials.

- Invite individuals to attend the following week and encourage them to attend the Primary Level open meeting.

- After the first meeting, meet with the core support group members and make any necessary adjustments to the meeting format.

Ongoing Management of the Living Free Program

- Have regularly scheduled meetings with the congregational care or support group pastor to evaluate the progress of the groups.

- Assist the pastor in keeping current on recovery ministry information through news articles, books and conferences.

- Inform the pastor of any situation involving a program participant which may require referral to a professional counselor because of their behavior or actions.

- Conduct facilitator briefings prior to the regularly scheduled meetings. This is a time to prepare announcements, review materials to be covered and to introduce prospective and regular facilitators to the process of conducting the meetings and appropriately handling matters that may arise. See page 34 for a review of *Facilitator Qualifications and Responsibilities*.

■ Make regular announcements of the courses being offered and publicize them several weeks before the meeting is to begin.

■ Have regular introductory meetings to provide an overview of the program and announce courses that are being offered.

■ Determine how voluntary financial contributions from the Living Free groups will be used. Consideration may be given to rent, child care, buying books for a recovery library, etc.

■ Ask participants to complete a class evaluation (see Appendix) prior to the final meeting of a particular course. Summarize the responses and review the information with the pastor and other facilitators.

Sample Announcements

Living Free Program Introduction
Program Overview

The _____ Church is offering the Living Free Program for people who were raised in an emotionally repressive or dysfunctional family. The goal of this ministry is to promote personal growth and spiritual enrichment for individuals who are seeking recovery from the traumas of their past. The program curriculum is based on the twelve-step process as a spiritual discipline with an emphasis on Christ-centered recovery. The program assists people in establishing and maintaining a loving relationship with God, themselves and others, and provides a safe environment where they can share their thoughts and feelings. With the grace of God, they can move from pain and denial toward healing and wholeness.

Living Free Program sessions are offered on four ascending levels. The curricula includes materials for individuals just beginning recovery, as well as for people in recovery who are familiar with twelve-step programs. Each level helps individuals increase self-esteem and cope with problems that affect their lives. Program participants can gain valuable insight about themselves, as they identify and confront significant issues in their lives.

Course Schedule

At this time, we are offering the following courses at the indicated times. For further information contact the church office.

Date   **Course**

_____ Primary Level Open Meeting (Weekly)
_____ When I Grow Up...I Want To Be An Adult
_____ The Truth Will Set You Free
_____ The Twelve Steps for Christians (Repeats every 13 weeks)
_____ The Twelve Steps—A Spiritual Journey

55

Meeting Announcement

What: Course Topic

When: Date   June 4, 1992   Time   7:00 PM

Where: 123 "A" Street, Room 40, San Diego

Who: Person to contact for questions — Mary Jones

Meeting Descriptions

Primary Level: Open Meeting

The Primary Level meetings are conducted weekly on an ongoing basis. Individuals are invited to attend these meetings before making a commitment to the more structured meetings in Levels One, Two and Three. These meetings are helpful for individuals who are just beginning recovery. They may still be identifying codependency or adult child issues and are not ready to make a commitment to participate in the more structured program.

Level One: Introduction to Recovery Issues

Level One introduces individuals to fundamental issues common to people in the beginning stages of recovery. The text offers wisdom and encouragement through emphasis on solid biblical principles.

Book used: **When I Grow Up...I Want To Be An Adult**

A ten-week course presenting foundation material for adults who suffer from wounded childhoods. It explores ways to discover our child-like nature and provides guidelines for Christ-centered recovery groups. The objective is to bring our healing home to family, friends and loved ones.

Book used: **The Truth Will Set You Free**

A twelve-week course for adults who were reared in an addictive or dysfunctional family. It includes a video program with a companion workbook designed to help Christians work through unresolved grief and codependency issues in a gentle, loving way.

Level Two: Introduction to the Twelve-Step Recovery Process

Level Two is an introduction to the Twelve Steps as a spiritual discipline and demonstrates the compatibility between Christianity and the Twelve Steps.

Book used: **The Twelve Steps for Christians**

The objective of the course is to discover the healing power of the twelve-step process when worked within a Christian perspective. The material is written for individuals who experienced trauma or some type of deprivation in their childhood.

Level Three: Twelve-Step Recovery

Level Three is an extensive 28-week course that presents the twelve-step process as a spiritual journey toward healing from childhood traumas and self-defeating behaviors.

Book used: **The Twelve Steps—A Spiritual Journey**

This course requires that participants read each chapter and answer questions prior to attending the weekly meetings. The text contains weekly exercises for use within small group settings. Biblical references aid Christians in confronting their past and surrendering their lives to God as part of their recovery journey.

Primary Level
Meeting Format

Opening Comments:

"Welcome to Living Free, a fellowship of the _____ recovery ministry. My name is _____, and I am _____ (a codependent, alcoholic/addict, etc.) recovering in this program."

"Please join me for a moment of silence, after which we will recite the Serenity Prayer."

Serenity Prayer

God, grant me the serenity
to accept the things I cannot change,
the courage to change the things I can,
and the wisdom to know the difference.
Living one day at a time,
enjoying one moment at a time,
accepting hardship as a pathway to peace;
taking, as Jesus did,
this sinful world as it is,
not as I would have it;
trusting that You will make all things right
if I surrender to your will;
so that I may be reasonably happy in this life
and supremely happy with You forever in the next.
Amen.

Reinhold Niebuhr

"If there is anyone here for the first time, please raise your hand and give us your first name so we can greet you."

"As children we often felt rejected when we openly expressed our needs. As adults, we often deny the reality of our past, and cannot see the dysfunctional behavior we have developed to repress our feelings. Rather than risking rejection today, many of us medicate our feelings through addictive/compulsive behaviors such as work, food, sex, religion, relationships, or alcohol and other drugs."

"By working the Twelve Steps, we gain the help, comfort and courage to look at the past, deal with it honestly and progress in our recovery journey with Jesus Christ. We believe that living "one day at a time" is Christian living at its best. May you find in this fellowship of discovery and recovery a life that is abundant, honest, joyous and free."

"I've asked _____ to read the Twelve Steps, and I've asked _____ to read the corresponding Bible verse for each Step."

"As your leader for this meeting, I will share for a few minutes, then will open the meeting for general discussion relating to the topic being covered. If you would like to share, please raise your hand to be recognized. Keep your sharing on recent experiences and events in your life. Focus on your personal strength and hope and limit your sharing to three to five minutes. This is a spiritually centered program, and we ask you to also share how your spirituality relates to the topic or the Step being discussed."

"The topic I've selected for this meeting is _____."

Closing Comments:

"Anonymity is the spiritual foundation of this program, ever reminding us to place principles above personalities. Whom you see here, what is said here, when you leave here, let it stay here, so that this meeting can be a safe place for us to speak honestly about our spiritual journey."

"This meeting is intended to supplement, not replace, other twelve-step meetings. We encourage you to attend other meetings that apply to your situation. We also support you in getting a sponsor and working the Steps, one day at a time."

"Living Free is a recovery program sponsored by this church as a way to introduce people to Christ-centered recovery. There are various courses of study offered throughout the year which include meetings for individuals at all levels of recovery. A calendar of these courses is available on the literature table. We encourage you to bring friends to this or to other Living Free meetings and invite them to experience some of the benefits that can be gained from participating in this program."

"Are there any recovery-related announcements?"

"Let us join hands and close with the Lord's Prayer."

Meeting format adapted from Recovery Works!

Meeting format adapted from Recovery Works!
The Rev. Stephen M. Smith, Director
2737 Buffalo Speedway, Suite 210
Houston, TX 77098-1004
(713) 621-2552

Chapter Seven

Working With a Recovery Partner

The Living Free Program has been developed to help individuals look at painful experiences from their past that are continuing to influence their lives today. Participants in the program have an opportunity to redefine their knowledge and understanding of themselves through writing about and sharing their progress in recovery. A Christ-centered version of the Twelve Steps, as adapted from Alcoholics Anonymous, is the foundational discipline used in the program.

Participants in the program often discover how their opinions of themselves and others have been founded on faulty information. This information is often passed on to them from parents, siblings and others who are unaware of their own worth and value, or the beauty of others.

Participants in all levels of the Living Free Program have an opportunity to see life through the eyes of an adult, rather than the eyes of a terrified, fearful and shame-filled child. They learn to stop viewing themselves as victims, accept the reality of their past and work toward enhancing the quality of their lives with the help of God's grace. The principal of Christ-centered partnership is exemplified in ECCLESIATES 4:9-12 *"Two are better than one, because they have a good return for their work; If one falls down, his friend can help him up. But pity the man who falls and has no one to help him up! . . . Though one may be overpowered, two can defend themselves. A cord of three strands is not quickly broken."*

A challenge often faced by participants is being willing to communicate with a "recovery partner" between meetings. A "recovery partner" is someone who can be trusted, and who will help an individual to recognize how denial can inhibit one's ability to discover the truth about themselves. Working with a recovery partner on a one-on-one basis makes it easier to identify the fears and resentments that are an after affect of the dysfunctional and addictive behavior.

Sharing with a "recovery partner" offers an opportunity to experience one-on-one relating without the distractions found when groups meet together. For individuals who have felt betrayed in the past, this is an opportunity for them to rebuild their trust. The dynamics of self-revelation (discovering exactly what one feels and thinks) can occur more easily through communicating with another trusted person. Through the process of sharing, something subtle and powerful happens that provides the courage to face reality and deal effectively with the fear of discovery.

Many people have difficulty overcoming the fear of revealing their true feelings. They may hide their fear by stating that they have nothing to offer. By communicating privately with a recovery partner they have an opportunity to develop mutual trust and reveal themselves to another person without feeling intimidated by others in a group setting. This dynamic can cause a breakthrough in learning to trust in someone and be willing to share openly about their life experiences.

Participating in the Living Free Program prepares individuals to become mentors to other people who are newly aware of their condition. They can demonstrate to others what they are learning for themselves and how the discipline of the Twelve Steps is strengthening their walk with God. By sharing their experience, strength and hope with others, they can grow, and at the same time help others to discover some of the joys they have discovered for themselves. By their continued commitment to work the Twelve Steps, face their character flaws, and through God's grace have them healed—they find others looking to them for comfort, direction and wisdom.

Choosing a Recovery Partner

A recovery partner is similar to a mentor and can be a role model for an individual who is learning how to enjoy a better quality of life through the love of God. It is important to choose someone who demonstrates qualities that are valued and respected.

These qualities include:

- a belief in the Christian faith and a willingness to demonstrate their walk with God.

- sincerity and honesty in sharing personal stories of recovery and how the Twelve Steps work in their lives.

- a willingness to provide support and encouragement by listening and giving honest feedback without trying to force change.

- an ability to confront difficult issues and ask for accountability in keeping commitments.

- openness of communication in all matters, even when discussing sensitive issues such as sexual abuse, violence, or other severe trauma-inducing subjects.

When choosing a recovery partner, it is advisable to select an individual who:

- shares common interests and experiences and demonstrates positive results in recovery.

- understands and identifies with the addictive, compulsive, or obsessive behavior that is being addressed (still encounters and is challenged by the behavior).

- has patience and compassion, is willing to listen attentively and offer suggestions without giving advice.

- is available to spend time together when it is necessary.

- is the same sex and can relate to personal issues in a non-threatening way.

Some questions and expectations that arise when choosing a recovery partner:

- What happens when one hears "No"?
  The process of dealing with fear of rejection can occur when asking someone to be a recovery partner. The program encourages rigorous honesty, and this is an opportunity to reveal to the other person the discomfort in asking to enter into a recovery partnership. By giving the other person freedom of choice, we can experience peace by detaching from the outcome of the request. This program is one where God works miracles. A recovery partnership may just "happen" as one participates in the recovery process.

- What happens when you are asked to be a partner and don't want to be?
  This program can assist one in more clearly understanding boundaries. Boundaries include how we spend our time, express our feelings and enter into new relationships. Knowing when to say "Thank you for asking, but that won't work for me," can be one of the important steps we take in simplifying our life, and does not require an explanation.

- What do you do when you grow out of the partnership?
  Ending a "recovery partner" relationship is part of learning to decide when to select more appropriate support and to know that one may not meet the needs of the recovery partner "forever." Personal growth is a natural part of the process. The outcome may still be a very good friendship.

Principles to Follow

The following principles have been adapted from the *Principles and Guidelines for Recovery Support Group Meetings* on pages 51-53, and include biblical references to support the statements.

■ Partners provide a non-threatening system of mutual accountability. For example, a partner can agree to call the other for support and prayer in abstaining from a harmful habit.

> *"Therefore confess your sins to each other and pray for each other so that you may be healed. The prayer of a righteous man is powerful and effective."* JAMES 5:14-16

■ Partners minister to each other's specific area of need with directed prayer each time they meet. Openly sharing thoughts and feelings helps to clarify needs in problem areas. This also contributes to being freed from the past to live honestly in the present with realistic expectations.

> *"Pray continually; give thanks in all circumstances, for this is God's will for you in Christ Jesus."*
> 1 THESSALONIANS 5:17 (NIV)

■ Partners encourage one another to progress from a state of physical, emotional and spiritual sickness to wholeness of life. Discomfort often takes place when unhealthy familiar behaviors are being transformed into new and healthy ones as we seek to do God's will.

> *"...consider how we may spur one another on toward love and good deeds."* HEBREWS 10:24 (NIV)

■ Partners aid one another in applying biblical truths to personal and relationship needs. When partners openly share their faults with one another, honesty, trust, and healing occur. This also means we can quote scripture to exemplify an experience.

> *"Jesus said,'If you hold to my teaching, you are really my disciples. Then you will know the truth, and the truth will set you free."* JOHN 8:31-32 (NIV)

Mutual Agreement Between Recovery Partners

A key part in establishing a relationship with a "recovery partner" is to reach an agreement on how the partners want to interact with one another.

The agreement can establish:

- what the expectations are between one another.
- the period of time in which the agreement will be in effect.
- specified times to evaluate the quality of the relationship.
- an understanding of how the relationship and/or agreement can be terminated.

The agreement is intended to encourage the partners to make a sincere effort to:

- Focus on the Twelve Steps and scripture as a tool to enhance one's relationship with God and others.

   Moving at one's own pace is important. At times there may need to be encouragement or confrontation when one has quit working the Steps. If a partner is unavailable or can't answer a question, seek out another twelve-step person to assist in understanding how they use this discipline in their recovery.

- Be available for phone calls or meeting in person.

   A key to success in recovery is making and keeping commitments. Having someone committed to being available may be something new and is an important part of honestly confronting discomfort. Willingness to ask for or offer support and encouragement helps to achieve healing and wholeness.

- Share my true feelings with my "recovery partner."

   Rigorous honesty is important when sharing feelings. Feelings require acknowledgement and appropriate expression without their being judged right or wrong. Selective disclosure when talking about feelings creates doubt between partners. Telling the truth by clearly identifying and sharing one's feelings supports healing.

■ Refrain from giving lengthy explanations when sharing.

Sharing is not intended to be a lengthy or dramatic recreation of personal stories. Referring to journal notes or workbook writing keeps the focus on the subject being shared and helps to avoid "intellectualizing" when sharing.

■ Complete the homework assignment each week.

Partners can provide support and encouragement to each other in completing the assignment. Sharing the results of homework writing often helps clarify the meaning of questions and is an opportunity to hear another perspective.

■ Spend a minimum of 15 minutes each day reading scripture, praying and meditating, including prayer for your recovery partner.

Prayer is talking to God, meditation is listening to God. Spending time in prayer and meditation can be a vital part of the recovery process. This is a spiritual program founded upon seeking to know God's will and experiencing His grace.

■ Respect confidentiality by refraining from disclosing information about my "recovery partner."

The effectiveness of this program is largely based on trust. Fear of gossip may prevent some people from honestly sharing the pain of their lives. Healing will be hindered unless there is trust that personal matters will remain confidential.

■ Accept some degree of discomfort as part of the healing process.

Some meetings may be painful when memories of certain events or hurtful feelings are recalled. It is important to have a "recovery partner" available to show compassion and be supportive as we confront painful issues. During the early stages of recovery it is advisable to accept discomfort and not be distracted by entering into new intimate sexual relationships.

- Support my "recovery partner" by listening attentively and giving him/her my undivided attention.

  Listening attentively and asking questions enables one to explore the options and possible courses of action. This can strengthen one another's ability to make healthy choices which foster suitable outcomes. This program does not include a plan to fix others and give unsolicited advice.

- Be kind to myself by accepting personal progress rather than perfection on this journey toward wholeness and seeking God's will.

  Recovery is a personal spiritual journey which is enriched by our personal relationship with God. Progress is not measured by the standards of others. Accepting progress rather than perfection can increase self-esteem by allowing mistakes to happen as part of growing.

- Not to overly spiritualize my sharing.

  Partners are not spiritual directors to each other or a source of advice which is more appropriately handled by clergy or a professional therapist. Use examples of how God is working without excessive emphasis on scripture. Keep the focus on one's own life as a way to illustrate how God's will is being done. This concept supports God's desire to relate to us on a deeply personal basis.

■ Focus on the Twelve Steps as a tool to enhance one's relationship with God and others.

At times there may need to be encouragement or confrontation when one has quit working the Steps. If a partner is unavailable or can't answer a question, seek out another twelve-step fellow traveler to assist in understanding how they use this discipline in their recovery. It is inappropriate to impose personal views on one's "recovery partner," particularly regarding one's relationship with God.

Final Thoughts

Being accepting of our "recovery partner" or others does not mean accepting addictive behavior slips or the rationalizations which follow. Being able to lovingly detach means not taking the behavior breakdown as a personal affront—that one has somehow failed the recovery partner.

Partners are not responsible for each other; their responsibility is to listen and respond from their own experience, strength and hope. Being heard by a trusted person helps us to work through the decision-making process.

Having a "recovery partner" may be a way to experience the unconditional love of God for the first time.

A sample of a Mutual Agreement Between Recovery Partners can be found in the Appendix, page 75.

Law Offices of
Treitler & Montisano

A Partnership of Professional Corporations
3737 Camino del Rio South, Suite 109
San Diego, California 92108

WILLIAM B. TREITLER
ANTHONY J. MONTISANO, JR.
BARRY E. HAGER

Telephone (619) 283-1111
Telecopier (619) 528-0746

April 25, 1991

Mr. Ron Halvorson
Recovery Publications
1201 Knoxville Street
San Diego, California 92110-3718

Dear Mr. Halvorson:

Per your request I am including a summary of my findings on the issue of potential liability for churches who are prospective participants in the Living Free program.

The key factor in preventing liability of the participating church in the program itself, and the individuals who are administrating the program, is to never hold the program out to be anything but a ministry, gathering group, or related function with the intent and purpose of providing spiritual guidance and spiritual support to the participants.

Do not use phraseology from psychiatrists and psychotherapists but instead use religious phraseology. For example, rather than using terms such as treatment, group therapy, consultations, counseling appointments and clients, use terms such as ministry, Bible group, prayer group, spiritual guidance and students.

It is also important that the participating students are not counseled to do a particular act or refrain from doing a particular act (e.g.: "Leave your drunken husband if he comes home again in that condition"). However, it would be appropriate to assist them in coping with a drunken husband by strengthening them spiritually.

As long as the program does not promote itself as a professional counseling program, and the people who instruct and meet with the students do not hold themselves out to be professional therapists of any kind, then the church, the program and instructors will not be held to a higher standard of care which the law assigns to professional therapists.

However, you must inform the instructors that although they will not be held to a professional standard of care (assuming they comply with the above advice), they must act resonably and avoid outrageous and egregious conduct.

If you have any questions regarding the above, or any other specific items or factual scenarios, please do not hesitate to contact me.

Very truly yours,

William B. Treitler

WBT:snt

71

Living Free
Congregational Survey

We are in the process of forming a recovery ministry to provide support and encouragement to interested members. If you are interested in participating in the programs that will be offered, please help us by completing this survey.

The survey is anonymous and will be used solely to determine the specific needs of the congregation members who wish to participate.

It is our sincere desire to create an environment where people can attend Christ-centered support group meetings as part of their commitment to heal their hurts.

Please check the behaviors that currently apply to you.

- Excessive use of drugs ( ) alcohol ( ) food ( ).

- Over-indulgence in sex ( ) work ( ) gambling ( ) spending ( ).

- Compulsive behavior expressed through excessive volunteering ( ) caretaking of others ( ) perfectionism ( ) self-improvement ( ).

- Obsessive focus on sin ( ) weight ( ) pornography ( ) status ( ) relationships ( ).

- Unreasonable fear of crowds ( ) rejection ( ) sex ( ) public speaking ( ) failure ( ).

- Excessive attention and focus placed on others as a means of establishing identity and self-worth ( ).

If you are in a relationship with someone who is not completing this survey, please check the behaviors that you feel apply to them.

- Excessive use of drugs ( ) alcohol ( ) food ( ).

- Over-indulgence in sex ( ) work ( ) gambling ( ) spending ( ).

- Compulsive behavior expressed through excessive volunteering ( ) caretaking of others ( ) perfectionism ( ) self-improvement ( ).

- Obsessive focus on sin ( ) weight ( ) pornography ( ) status ( ) relationships ( ).

- Unreasonable fear of crowds ( ) rejection ( ) sex ( ) public speaking ( ) failure ( ).

- Excessive attention and focus placed on others as a means of establishing identity and self-worth ( ).

Sample Agreement

Mutual Agreement
Between Recovery Partners

I, _____, agree to enter into a Recovery Partner agreement with _____, as a way to be supported and held accountable in dealing with behaviors that keep me from the best God has for me. I am seeking recovery from these ineffective patterns of behavior so that I may become more fully connected to God, myself and others.

I will make a sincere effort to:

- Focus on the Twelve Steps and scripture as a tool to enhance my relationship with God and others.

- Be available by phone or to meet in person.

- Share my true feelings with my "recovery partner."

- Refrain from giving lengthy explanations when sharing.

- Complete the homework assignment each week.

- Spend a minimum of 15 minutes each day reading scripture, praying and meditating, including specific prayer for my recovery partner.

- Respect confidentiality by refraining from disclosing information about my "recovery partner."

- Accept some degree of discomfort as part of the healing process.

- Support my "recovery partner" by listening attentively and giving him/her my undivided attention.

- Be kind to myself by accepting personal progress rather than perfection on my journey toward wholeness and seeking God's will.

- Not to overly spiritualize my sharing.

The term of this agreement is from_____
to _____.

   We agree to meet _____ (weekly, monthly, etc.) and
spend time reviewing the progress and compatibility of this
relationship. If, for any reason, either partner feels this relationship
does not serve his/her recovery needs, the agreement can be
terminated by notifying the other partner.

Signed:_____

Date:_____

Class Evaluation

Course Title: _____ Date: _____

Facilitator(s): _____
_____

As a participant in the Living Free support group program, your feedback is important. You can help to assure that the program design is having the desired effect of affirming and encouraging participants' recovery process. This anonymous evaluation form will assist in making changes that more fully meet the needs of future participants.

On a scale of 1 to 10 (10 being the most favorable response), please rank the following categories of the program. Your comments are also appreciated in response to the questions.

Effectiveness of Materials: Rank _____

How do you feel the materials assisted you in moving forward toward identifying and healing areas of concern in your life?

_____
_____
_____

Attentiveness to Ground Rules: Rank _____

What is your assessment of the value of ground rules as a tool for assisting the management of the group process? (i.e. no crosstalk or advice giving, completing the homework before each meeting, contacting another member of your family group for homework support.)

_____
_____
_____

Individual Progress: Rank _____

How would you rank your progress in identifying important issues that have negatively affected your life?

_____

_____

_____

Mutual Support: Rank _____

In what way did the small (family) group interactions affect your participation in the meetings, and in your ability to participate in the process of working the material?

_____

_____

_____

Facilitator Role: Rank_____

How did you feel about having a fellow recovering peer functioning as the Living Free facilitator? What suggestions do you have for this person to enhance their effectiveness in that role?

_____

_____

_____

The Twelve Steps
of Alcoholics Anonymous

Step One—We admitted we were powerless over our separation from God—that our lives had become unmanageable.

Step Two—Came to believe that a Power greater than ourselves could restore us to sanity.

Step Three—Made a decision to turn our will and our lives over to the care of God *as we understood Him.*

Step Four—Made a searching and fearless moral inventory of ourselves.

Step Five—Admitted to God, to ourselves and to another human being the exact nature of our wrongs.

Step Six—Were entirely ready to have God remove all these defects of character.

Step Seven—Humbly asked Him to remove our shortcomings.

Step Eight—Made a list of all persons we had harmed and became willing to make amends to them all.

Step Nine—Made direct amends to such people wherever possible, except when to do so would injure them or others.

Step Ten—Continued to take personal inventory and when we were wrong promptly admitted it.

Step Eleven—Sought through prayer and meditation to improve our conscious contact with God *as we understood Him*, praying only for knowledge of His will for us and the power to carry that out.

Step Twelve—Having had a spiritual awakening as the result of these steps, we tried to carry this message to others, and to practice these principles in all our affairs.

The Twelve Traditions of Alcoholics Anonymous

One—Our common welfare should come first; personal recovery depends upon A.A. unity.

Two—For our group purpose there is but one ultimate authority—a loving God as He may express Himself in our group conscience. Our leaders are but trusted servants; they do not govern.

Three—The only requirement of A.A. membership is a desire to stop drinking.

Four—Each group should be autonomous except in matters affecting other groups of A.A. as a whole.

Five—Each group has but one primary purpose—to carry its message to the alcoholic who still suffers.

Six—An A.A. group ought never endorse, finance or lend the A.A. name to any related facility or outside enterprise, lest problems of money, property and prestige divert us from our primary purpose.

Seven—Every A.A. group ought to be fully self-supporting, declining outside contributions.

Eight—Alcoholics Anonymous should remain forever nonprofessional, but our service centers may employ special workers.

Nine—A.A., as such, ought never be organized, but we may create service boards or committees directly responsible to those they serve.

Ten—Alcoholics Anonymous has no opinion on outside issues; hence the A.A. name ought never be drawn into public controversy.

Eleven—Our public relations policy is based on attraction rather than promotion; we need always maintain personal anonymity at the level of press, radio and films.

Twelve—Anonymity is the spiritual foundation of all our Traditions, ever reminding us to place principles before personalities.

Bibliography

Books

Friends in Recovery. *The Twelve Steps—A Spiritual Journey.* San Diego: Recovery Publications, Inc., 1988.

May, Gerald *Addiction and Grace.* New York: Harper & Row, 1988.

McGinnis, Jack and Shlemon, Barbara. *The Truth Will Set You Free.* San Diego: Recovery Publications, Inc., 1991.

Ross, Ron. *When I Grow Up. . .I Want To Be An Adult.* San Diego: Recovery Publications, Inc., 1991.

Ryan, Dale & Juanita. *Recovery from Addictions.* Downers Grove: Inter-Varsity Press, 1990.

Washton, Arnold & Boundy, Donna. *Willpower's Not Enough: Understanding and Recovering From Addictions of Every Kind.* New York: Harper & Row, 1989.

Monographs

Bear, Gordon. "Church Support Groups, What They Are, When You Need Them, and How to Get Them Started." *Baptist General Conference Women's Ministries.*

Ryan, Dale S. "Promises and Pitfalls of Congregation-based Support Groups." *The National Association for Christian Recovery.*

Order Form

9908	Living Free	_____	$ 5.95	_____
9906	New Clothes from Old Threads	_____	$ 9.99	_____
9907	The Truth Will Set You Free (Workbook)	_____	$10.95	_____
9007	The Truth Will Set You Free (Book & Video)	_____	$99.95	_____
9902	The 12 Steps for Adult Children	_____	$ 7.95	_____
9901	The 12 Steps—A Way Out	_____	$14.95	_____
9904	The Twelve Steps for Christians	_____	$ 7.95	_____
9903	The Twelve Steps—A Spiritual Journey	_____	$14.95	_____
9905	When I Grow Up...I Want To Be An Adult	_____	$12.95	_____

Subtotal _____

*Sales Tax _____

**Shipping & Handling _____

(U.S. Funds Only) TOTAL _____

Visa and **MasterCard** Accepted

Bankcard No.
_____

Expiration Date
_____

Signature
_____

* California residents add applicable sales tax.

COD orders—add an additional $4.00

** Shipping and Handling:
Minimum Charge $3.75
Orders over $25.00—$5.50
Orders over $55.00, add 10% of Subtotal.

To Order by Phone: (619) 275-1350 or (800) 873-8384
To Order by FAX: (619) 275-5729

Or send this order form and a check or money order for the total to:

Recovery Publications, Inc.
1201 Knoxville Street
San Diego, CA 92110-3718

Name: _____

Address: _____

City/State/Zip: _____

Phone: _____